It's What He Would've Wanted

FROM THE AUTHOR OF

From the Author of (2000)

Nonsense (2003)

Back with the Human Condition (2016)

Dandy Bogan: Selected Poems (2018)

Moral Sloth (2019)

The Stupefying (2022)

IT'S WHAT HE WOULD'VE WANTED

Nick Ascroft

Te Herenga Waka University Press
Victoria University of Wellington
PO Box 600 Wellington
teherengawakapress.co.nz

First published 2025

A catalogue record is available at the National Library of New Zealand

ISBN 978-1-77692-293-2

Printed in Singapore by Markono Print Media Pte Ltd

For all the dead.

Contents

LITTLE HELP

The Drunken Hedge

(for Ashleigh)

The drunken hedge stumbles
into you as you make your driveway
and you lie there and sleep, five minutes,

seven minutes.
After whatever unconscious period of minutes –
though you drag yourself back up to half-mast

and swing indoors –
part of you will always remain asleep
at the base of the hedge, and forever raising yourself

up out of it, thinking, well I was asleep there.
Tunnelling inside and into bed, your
carefulness drunk too but still careful,

the ceiling turns
with the sound of his sleep breathing, heavy and long
with the out-breaths, whispers and whistles

on the in.
All of your mouth sounds are loud.
The inner cheek sucks and squelches.

There is a piece of olive wedged behind a canine
your tongue works at like an octopus.
The heartbeat in your ears is tympanic,

signalling tone shift.
At work the next week you are still asleep in a bush
and, realising, stagger inside, mud on your forehead,

a leaf in your fringe.
The pillow bristles and you disappear,
reappearing horizontal on the driveway verge,

thinking, here I am then.

Bad Cookbooks

Dinner for None

**

Dark Night of the Soup

**

Carcinogenic Treats

**

So So Easy but You're Taking Ages

**

What in the Jellied Hell? Aspics

**

Body and Blood of Christmas

**

Hill of Beans

**

Barf Bag Fingerpaint

**

The Kid Is Wailing in Hunger

**

Nuclear Fusion

**

Feed the Rich

**

Divorced Dad Smorgasbord

**

Mother Fudger

**

Cannibalism for Beginners

**

No It's Tasty

**

Cooking with Guts

**

Cook a Doodle Don't

**

If It's Brown, Wolf It Down

**

The Joyless Diet

**

Fish from Bins: Dumpster Diving Suppers

**

Sous-Cheffing for Back-Seat Drivers

**

Not Like That

**

Force-Fed Kale

**

Ready Steady Google It

**

Salmon-Hell-Yeah

**

It's All Protein!

**

Roughage for Nana

**

Winner Winner Mushroom-Based Yoghurt

**

Can Opening for Cretins

**

I'll Have What She's Having: Horse Tears

**

How to Eat Your Feelings

**

Gruel?

**

Wet Market Bats

**

Blubber!

**

Edible Vests

**

Slop!?

**

Hate-Cooking for Your Idiot

**

Unidentifiable Matter

**

Upcycled Cat Biscuits

**

Grey Gravies of Great Britain

**

Just Boil It

**

Through a Straw

**

Lick It Up

**

Bite Me

The Centaur for Woman

. . . is a 1990s fillum
featuring Al Pacino
as a blind centaur.
Whenever his nostrils
fill with the stench
of Gabrielle Anwar he neighs
a wild: *Hoo-ah! Hoo-ah!*
Are you back to the
empty wordplay, Ascroft?
What happened to all
the harrowing verse
about your separation?
Old hat.
The mulling I mull on now,
the mull I return to
like the Mull of Kintyre
or the Mulligatawny,
the mulling I mull around
and around
like a mulberry bush,
the mulling I mull like wine,
the whinneying I whine
like poor blind
Al Pacino the centaur
or poor Gabrielle Anwar
billowing plumes of whiff
that the horses of the world
gad up on two legs over
is this,
the sensual word mill.
The centre for yeomen.

The senator for Wyoming.
The sensible Roman.
The scent of a brrm-brrm.
This end of a footman.
The sativa! Whoa man!
There went off a snowman.
The sniff of a werewolf.
The woof of an earwig.
An elf and her falafel.
The piffle, only as effervescent
as it is evanescent.
One small step for man,
one giant leap for
the scent of a woman.
Cometh the hour,
cometh the centaur.
Cometh the *hoo-ah*,
cometh the pitter patter
of a little baby batter.

Another Poem with a Found Feather

Another poem with a tūī going nuts in a kōwhai.
Another poem with a kid, eyeballs strangled mid-epiphany.
Another poem with incongruous vocabulary.
Another with a day moon, clubbed by analogy.
Another agog at the vastness and opacity of the inner planet, the intolerable kilometres of tight hot sludge.
Another strewn with fuckery.
Another with the author spraying terror from their pupils on the kitchen window vista.
Another with a line they will unwrite, rewrite, revert and torment themselves with until dead or insensible.
Another poem of longing.
Another poem with a loose end.
Another with an end that refers too neatly to the start.
A cat.
Two ducks.
A fucking pūkeko.
The seasons – blowing – plummeting – choking on smoke – as still as a lake.
Everything half-lit, everything slow, the shadows described in Latinate puffery.
Another poem shouted into the ears of this peacock ex-lover.
Another's unpunctuated bamboozlement.
Another with   empty stomach.
Another poem naming:

- — Philips, Nassers, Jocastas
- — people that have clearly been made up or misunderstood
- — people you are supposed to know or care about
- — Greeks
- — terminology, nomenclature, designations

—   screeches you can't unhear
—   an unnameable scent.
Another poem as useless at music as a penny whistle.

Thing

O the infamy one indulges,
John Ashbery style, as one drubs
through bronze suburbs,
only to putter to a disarray,
cycle skidding into the same
dead-end utility holes.

**

Nobody likes an autodidact,
or a multi-instrumentalist.
They make the rest of us look like lazy
hunchbacks.
But here I am.

**

All I want for Christmas is to be sour
and petty.

**

And look at you. The state.

I can intuit the offness.
I can sense through the ether
that you are feeling off
via your full body cast.
What is it now?
Whatever it is I will bear it.

You can tell me. I'm from
the time before people cared about things.

Just settle on a single grievance
for the love of bleeped-out fuck.
Stop sloshing about like doubloons
in a sailor's pocket.

**

My drinking. I would only call it that –
my drinking – if I were motivated
by grandiosity and I am.
Though I may look like a slug and
cycle like a slug I am Oscar Wilde.
The Oscar Wilde of Otago and Southland.

A grand mollusc am I.
My drinking includes milk,
tea comma biscuit-dunked
and electrolyte tablets comma in solution.
Henceforward termed, so as not to mislead:
my slurping.

**

The hut, it needs mud and reeds.
The cut that bleeds blood, it bleeds.

**

I am saying this poem to myself at night and
not writing down any of it.
What difference would it make if I did?

Beast That Needs to Be Tamed

The imagination is a beast
that needs to be tamed.
It doesn't want to work, but if you force it to work
it will.
You can't bribe it.
The flattery and seduction that you think
sells elsewhere does not for definite here.
You can coax it out too.
Let it have the reins for a little.
Let it bumble around
on its own accord.
What's the worst
that could find itself into print?

YOUR FUNERAL

It's What He Would've Wanted

When I die I want as little fuss as possible, no grave, just a small utilitarian series of pyramids.

When I die bury me inside my own head. As in life so in death.

When I die or if I die, and at the moment immortality looks the more likely option, you may have to reverse back over me a few times to be sure, while howling for me to please shut up.

If I die on bin day, take the win.

Do not stand at my grave and fry a truffled omelette served on rye.

If I should die before I wake, I pray my soul is sweet as cake. If I should wake before I die, I pray the thing is tough and dry.

When I die do not cremate me in a flame-retardant bodysuit 'as a joke'.

When I die take solace in the fact my agonies are over and that I am at peace or writhing on a lake of fire.

If I die before returning your favourite casserole dish, and you toss and turn at night wondering if it will be cunty to raise it with my executor, or if you could just sneak into my apartment and take it, but imagine if my son was there and caught you in the act, regarding you sideways with his silver and sorrowful eyes, or you could wait for a reasonable length of time, risking the casserole dish's disbursement elsewhere, please be still. You know me. Please recognise it's what I would've wanted that you suffer.

‘When you die,’ you say to me in a kind voice, ‘your wishes will no longer matter, so let us do whatever we want to honour you.’ I would reply that I am touched but you are pressing too tightly to my face the pillow.

When I die and am reincarnated as a Manchester United fan, kill me.

The two chocolate coins you had slipped onto my eyes as a prank were in fact very pleasing to Charon the ferryman. He mimed eating them with his pointy teeth and we both had a great laugh. He couldn’t let me aboard of course.

If my funeral planner is reading this wondering what I would’ve wanted, appreciate that I would not have wanted a funeral planner. A funeral, sure, but last-minute bedlam. Where’s the body? I thought Leah was sorting the hearse? Etc.

When I die do prod me with a broom, just on the chance.

Should it turn out that, as would make a lot of sense if we’re honest, there is no afterlife, please continue to believe I am watching over you and scowling.

If you never had a chance to say goodbye, say it now. Put down the defibrillators.

If you never had a chance to tell me that you loved me, I am aware it is because you were more meh on me.

If in the last ten years of my life you struggled with my dementia, and can now only remember me that way, tiresome and screaming obscenities, think now of the younger spryer self who wrote this, equally exhausting and obscene.

The only noble death is by misadventure, inshallah.

In life I was haunted by regret, so in death I will flip the roles and haunt it back.

I will haunt chip shops, refrigerators jammed with V, Wellington Indoor Sports, tile bags, the bars and the beer halls and the public houses, and then I will die.

Enjoy, etymology nerds, the irony that death will save us from the constant mortification.

Bury me in a scoop of chips, as in life so in etc.

Don't bury my delusions of grandeur. They must continue to walk the earth, crowds pouring out of houses to cheer them on, saluted by sailors, curtsied at by wenches.

When I die and they lay me to rest, you're gonna go to a place that's depressed. When I lay me down to die, I'm gonna recommend you drink some spirits with a guy.

Oh my darling, oh my darling, oh my darling, Clementine. You are lost and gone forever. Or I lovebombed and you blocked me.

Do not throw yourself on my pyre. Throw your better-looking friend.

Stop all the clocks. Cease production on those despicable Apple Watches.

Plywood coffin, old Persil box, sleeping bag and duct tape, a pile of leaves, entire city of Dunedin transformed into my personal necropolis, whatever my pride can bear.

Place a thing for safekeeping in my coffin, such as a feather or my browsing history.

Bury me on one of the many hills I have died on.

Bury me in a joke pushed too far.

Bury me arse up.

When I die I would like this poem read out at my funeral because I think it would be funny, or funny at first and then misjudged.

Pastiche for Mum

Do not stand at my grave and cry.
I am not there. I'm in Dubai.
Don't stand and bulge your bottom lip.
Sit down, you'll only hurt your hip.
Don't slump though as you sit and stare
In fact, get up. You're in my chair.
I'm wind, I'm gulls, the warmth of sun,
the pinkish icing on a bun.
When blinded by the glare of day,
qu'est que j'ai dit? What did I say?
At my grave, don't pout and gurn.
I am not there. I'm in this urn.

Fair-Weather Friend

(for Niki)

Shuffling down to work in the freezing
rain, I'm trying to remember everything
I can about my lost friend
before the data fade. I don't store
visual memories well. I can't
remember excerpts of verbatim speech.
I hold on to gists,
locations, music.
We were marching down George Street once,
and she had a new song in her head
I didn't yet know: No one
as dope as her, she sang. Outkast.
I crooned along, copying.
My umbrella blows inside out
at the crossing now, showering
some fellow crosser with the droplets gathered
on its surface. Their face is
how I feel. I twist windward
to let it blow back into shape.
The umbrella, not the face.
There were many long
drives, and me in the passenger seat, bleating
away. I can't picture her. I remember
nothing she said.
In the Subaru once we drove
to Westport. On the tape player, Missy
Elliott listed types of boys: black, white,
Puerto Rican, Chinese.
Then she would join in:
'Why dai dai oh doy oh dai oh dai.'

Across from big orange St Paul's now
someone is screaming
with righteous anger into their phone:
You can fuckin' well just,
and then they are cut
off. I cross again and walk in the parliament
grounds. In my head with each
plod: nobody dope
as me. The saddest of all brag-songs today.
At lunchtime walking to the hygienist, the rain
still chilling but spitty
now: ain't nobody dope.
Lying quietly in the chair, as the hygienist
works a tiny buzzing blade
against a bright nerve in my gum line,
my eyes squeeze closed. Chinese
boys. I make a mental
note to contact her ex-boyfriend Aaron Chow
and tell him of her passing.
I remember what she wrote. When
she called herself 'Wifey' in a note to me,
and my girlfriend didn't find it
funny. The last thing she emailed:
'Get on with it Ascroft.'
I had promised to send all the latest
gossip and complaints. Never
got to it. Didn't get on with it in time.
She needed money. Louise
had made that clear. But
I never got to it.
Once, she transferred a thousand dollars to me
like it was nothing. The dead
can't forgive, but I am abominable
enough to forgive myself.

Poem for Your Funeral 5

When this guy lived, he was a pain.
But now he's dead and down the drain.
He used to drone, each story long,
how he was never in the wrong.
But now he's dead, the bucket kicked,
his eyes look like eggs Benedict.
His lips are still. He can't be heard.
And so I get the final word.

Mum's Second-Most Magnificent Tumble on the Way to an Eye Appointment

Mum called a taxi. But despite herself,
high-stepping through the verge before the footpath
in jandals, with the morning dew a foot bath,
she capsized and could not right herself.
At last, it shambled in, the taxi, idling
while it waited, Mum so low the driver
couldn't spot her. Low, but a survivor,
she began to yell. He started sidling
off. HELP! HELP! She called. He paused. HELP ME!
It waited there. And then began to pull
away again. HELP! HELP! Her yelp at full
intensity broke through. He turned his key.
Once found, he got her up. Did she need aid?
'Let's go! To the optometrists!' she bayed.

The Time I Shook Allen Curnow's Huge Paw

The title says it all, and says or least
implies that you, too young, too wispy small,
did not detain that literary beast
as heedlessly he crossed you in the hall.
The book awards it was, and I was all
magnificent in penguin suit with Helen
Clark behind, Karl Stead beside, who needed
wine, and so, the grin across my melon
just too impish, our PM conceded,
faux-aghast that I had centipeded
in to snatch a red from off her table.
So gigantic – Timaru's Clark Gable –
as Curnow passed I shot up like a bloom.
And oh the time I talked at Keri Hulme.

BIG ASK

Big If

Owen felt fancy in a bar the owners called a speakeasy, despite alcohol not being illegal, and the bouncer indicating the open door with his thumbs.

The bouncer whispered into his walkie talkie: note to self, get Handee towels.

Some cocktails need to be shaken after you've popped out your cufflinks and rolled up your ridiculous sleeves.

Seven floors up, me and the kid chucked a dart each out the window. Mine plummeted harmlessly into a dog. His caught the wind and sailed beyond time and reckoning to the driveway.

Sticks and stones, etc. Names will never hurt you unless you have one like Rudolph or Enid that is just too easy a target for light artillery.

A snakebite is a drink we used to request before the war. Cider, beer and a squirt of raspberry laid over a colossal grief at the impotence of your central thesis.

By the time you finished your PhD we all had jetpacks and futuristic haircuts. You had a potato sack and a half a toothbrush.

It's not that the idiots won. We just won *this time*. If there's a single thing that's universally true, it's that we all lose in the end. Take comfort in the fact that I will fall to my knees, blood gurgling out my neck and a baffled look across my face, some lime pickle still on a poppadom in my left hand.

Take comfort in shoes. Take comfort in short breaths. Take comfort out on the town and show it the most soulless bars on Courtenay Place.

Before the revolution came I was already up against the wall, pashing some middle-aged stick that would turn out to be my second cousin.

There are few things I take pride in, but who else can peel a hot egg like me and not get upset about it.

If I am smug, it is only a refuelling stop on the way to humility. See the whole journey, not the arsehole.

Even those guys with the hats don't believe in redemption anymore.

Which hats, you ask, hoping against hope. Just hats. All hats. A vagueness of hats with no specificity to rest your mind's eye on.

Baseball caps? Not impossible. Sectarian hats? <background cicada buzz>

You repeat it: Sectarian hats? I would answer, but what are sectarian hats that mark them out against the multitude of hats oozing in and out of focus, among all the world's throng of hats and the strange heads they sit atop?

Owen was easily distracted if there was a bee about.

Bigger Ask

Kiss me Winnie.
Dream on, Brynn.
Kiss me like you'd kiss the left hook

from a drunken plumber.
Kiss me like you kissed Mrs Winnie
at the wedding under a paper lantern

while your dad blubbed.
Kiss me like rain kisses
the deck of a tugboat,

like a barnacle kisses and won't unkiss,
like fire kisses hair,
like an egg kisses the flat

of a cop's forehead and drools.
Kiss me like you're thirsty enough
and a kiss is rum eggnog.

Kiss me like you'd kiss a horse
goodnight.
Kiss me like a horse

a carrot,
all lips and teeth.
Peck me like a chicken.

Kiss me like light does
a cubic zirconia.
Kiss me like Debbie does

Dallas.
Kiss me like Alice in Wonderland.
Kiss me like a migraine kisses

the right side of your seeing
with fractal lightning
and your will to live.

Kiss me tender.
Kiss me hardy.
Get a grip.

Have a Little Style

There's a blackbird above the city – high
– fluttering and bombing
over the shadow-glassed turrets of make-work
while all the others are shoved
in their oaks and gum trees,

bottom-heavy little blackbirds, nictitating
at the bland trunks they are squashed
against. You think I mean
be like it, the arse-troubling blackbird in the city's loft?
Jesus. It is indubitably a wanker.

Look at it, boring rhythmic gymnast. Affectatious.
It is
a dingbat. But you should have a little style.
Those dreadful old swing guys had something.
You could be an excellent prick.

Still saluting like an A-plus prefect?
Bravissimo. You are very good
at the local line. In ten years
it will be another thing again and you'll do it dutifully.
And when I say you, I'm firing one inwards.

<Stares out apartment windows> Beautiful.
The mountains. The flat sea.
I have no opinion that I am not
recycling from
someone else without realising it.

But you could have a little style.

Dire Dairy

Dear Diary. All the best poems begin that way,
signalling the things you would only admit
to yourself: the horrible truths, the confessions
of scandal, matters of loathing, matters of love.
The worst too. Keep it to yourself hey. If you
don't have the grace to dolly it up for Mike and

Myrtle Reader, better to abandon it to the vault.
Now every visit to the hygienist reminds me
of Niki. I went the day after she died and wrote
that grief dump poem from a few pages ago.
Now the line haunts me. I was back again
yesterday and missing her. My hygienist, Helen,

used to be so gentle around the gum line.
I would compliment her. Never have I had so
gentle yet effective a hygienist. But the years
are insidious. Helen has become not callous
but inured to the pain of others. 'Are you still
doing . . . playing that . . . game?' 'Scrabble?'

'That's it.' Helen has remembered me and even
if I am this titbit of factoid to her and no more
beyond the food trap in the only remaining
wisdom tooth, I am happy to have been retained
in her mind. A ridiculous thing I miss in Niki's
absence, I realise, while Helen is being not

callous around the gum line, is someone
witnessing my life, someone I would have to
explain my decisions to, someone to

entertain with my pratfalls and bronze medals.
Not straight away, but at some point, I would
need to recount what had transpired since

I saw her last as a story and one that she would
question if she thought I was skipping around
a thing or lying. It's a selfish thing to miss, but
I am the only one here and can be as selfish as
I like in my missing. I miss the feeling of her
judgement hanging over my choices, the thought

she might shake her head and say, Ascroft, oh.
I miss most, and even more selfishly, the person
I can confess to, the person eager to hear about
my love life, or what might pass for it, or what
I might imagine for it. Instead . . . Dear Diary.
Friends are good to have because they are mostly

easy. The relationship is near static. It grows,
your knowledge of each other and the comfort
of your manner, but the essential tenor once
established is fixed, or fixed enough not to feed
anxiety, or too much anxiety. The other type of
relationship though, as I feel myself having

the feelings and creating fantastical stories in
my head, the kind from daft storylines of films,
is a shitshow. Love is for young people with its
self-deceit and cross purposes. A young man in
love may make us feel a bit sick, but the crush of
a middle-aged man makes us wince. Still, the

feelings remain, driving as direct towards
the self-deceit and cross purposes as ever.
To me they half-feel noble, gemlike, urges of
kindness and care. The eyes narrow on suspicion,
it's a story I need to tell myself. Men tell
themselves stories about love that are designed

to bolster, to make themselves think they are
good. There's desire too. It's interwoven
into the thing but is less interesting to poke at.
Desire is the yowling of cats, incomprehensible
but straightforward. If the love makes you wince,
the desire makes you shrug. Even if disgusted,

it's a shrug of disgust. Even if intrigued, it's
a shrug of intrigue. Dour Diary. The thing I
would like to confess, one rung down from
desire, one rung up from love, one leap from
the entire rope ladder, is bravery. It takes
bravery to throw oneself at someone. I don't mean

my hygienist, but imagine it. Frisbeeing the bib
off my chest, swatting off the sunglasses and
. . . what? Lunging? Or, backtracking please,
it takes bravery to flirt. The bravery to see
the little wince at your attempt, and the bravery
to think you could have misread the wince so

issuing out more of it, gritting the teeth and
emitting a barrage of the flirting. Whatever that is
and whatever it might mean I have no idea,
having never successfully been suggestive.

And. Receiving the wince again, clearer this time.
Unmistakable? Well that's a high bar. All

expressions are mistakable. It's conceivable
that even the most pee-yew wince could have
been something else. It could have been she was
haunted in an unrelated flash by a memory.
She could have had a stomach pain. It might have
been tinnitus. One more slog up Mount Bravery.

One more blurted essaying of intimation. We all
have the ability. There is a version of ourselves
where we might say it, or say it with a look.
There would be relief at least in saying it,
wince or no wince, to not be stuck swinging from
the rope ladder. It's the thing I would most like

to confess. Bravery.

Still, There's Honour in Not Bothering Anyone

It would be rude to mention you are trapped in the organ pipe during the recital. Or, now that you didn't at the start of it, and we're fifteen minutes in, well.

It would be rude to put your hand up to ask about a tissue for the bleeding nose while Tania is having a seizure.

I would feel uncomfortable to ruin this candlelit dinner by getting down on one knee.

Everyone else in the theatre starts applauding at the end. The stitches in her palm are still fresh and the wound tender. (She had only tried to catch the chainsaw because it was her husband's favourite.) Everyone else is applauding though. She scans the rows looking for one renegade or double amputee. Making the right face, she could point to the bandage. What face is that? The universally recognised face for 'I can hardly clap with this can I'. It would seem quite a performance. Who would she be doing it for? She doesn't know these people. And think of it, her desperation broadcast to all. The absolute shiver. Simpler to bite the lip and clap a little. As shouts of 'Encore! Encore!' bubble up from happy normal concertgoers, the applause builds.

It would be rude to question the bill.

This isn't what I ordered, I mumble with my eyes, once their back is turned.

This isn't my child, you want to tell the nurse at the neonatal unit. Never has anyone's frown looked so exhausted. She just needs rest and at least this one is alive.

You only climbed inside the organ pipe because she was so distraught, the nurse or the woman you should've proposed to or little Tania. She'd dropped her gran's ring in there and it was all over. With its limited crawlspace and your general troll-shaped weirdness, you hadn't wanted to climb into the organ pipe. But the world divides into two people: people who will whistle an unaware whistle then recount a long anecdote about their file uploading with all their changes not having been saved – while Tania or whoever sobs and those who will crawl into an organ pipe to fetch a lost ring.

'There it is!' yells the nurse or whoever. 'It was by the foot pedals the whole time.'

The organist isn't even furious to be interrupted in the final bars. They laugh and pick it up. 'Encore!' howl the concertgoers and all applaud.

There is a moment in the hubbub when you could try to dislodge yourself and escape but there's something in the applause. Distress. A muffled whimpering. And then: Messiaen.

Gentleman of the Night

This is a less good poem.
I recommend skipping on to another.
But I realise why I like New Zealand music.
Not the culture of guitar chords
so much, by which I mean
that sense of fuzz and discord
wrapped in a tea towel.
More something obtuse and obvious.
That the strummer of it comes out of
the same paddock.

Do You Hear Yourself?

A plane is sucked into the sky.
As your eyes dart to a starling at a chimney
your awareness

describes it in a toneless sentence.
The voice in your head has no music.

No humming vowels and puffy consonants.
There's nothing guttural,
no scratching on the windpipe.

You claim to hear its music, hum and puff
though it has none:
a thing we call a voice that is not a voice.

The guitars squeak in your headphones.
The city haze fades lilac in the twilight.

We like to think there is a truth
in a contradiction.
It's how those of us with the auburn

neck-beard snatch at the purpose
of a Zen koan.
Logically there is a null.

A contradiction must,
misread as an equation,

cancel itself out completely
like two equal and opposite wave patterns,

leaving nothing but the truth that
one thing less itself is zero.
It's a cheap point to say that
language makes a spattered apron.

There is something
you are unaware of in your awareness.

It has a little voice.
The bird departs its chimney
and the voice has an opinion.

When you hear it, you wonder:

Is it always there?

And in the times I don't apprehend it,
how can it be there at all?

FUCK SAKE

Old Farts

Tonight, the women having gone, and just
the two of us there, playing one last game
of Scrabble, George will loose a held-in gust,
his customary fart barrage. The same
tub-bubbling of rasps and sour smells.
No longer needing to suppress them for
politeness sake, he'll parp the full church bells.
It's nice he doesn't fear distressing or
enraging the olfactory devices
of my nostrils. I'll say nothing much
and nor will he. A 'there you go' suffices.
Not for Rick. When George frees up the clutch –
and Rick is there – to let his arse unclench,
Rick's face will blanch. He'll retch: 'Fuck sake! The stench!'

Pig Magnet

I bike the kid six kilometres to school half
the week through a blizzard of fine weather,
or we take the bus. For that we tear ourselves
out the front door at 8am, elbows high

like geese, wrists aflap, had geese wrists
and elbows and the requisite terror
of being late. The lift lowers us
to the basement then carries us back up
to floor seven as we have forgotten the lot:

bags, batteries, keys, shreds of dignity,
senses of purpose and self-agency,
thunderheads of impotent huff, laptops,
sunhats, sunscreen, son, weeping now to be
so looked over by this calamity of fatherhood

I teeter in the half-on shoes of, belt
half-threaded, jersey over neck only, so far,
but a lot can be achieved as we plummet
down the lift shaft like manna from heaven
in the most

waft-paced
of all lifts,
plummeting
at one storey
every two

slow-counted
seconds

to the basement. Out drags the bike from the
under-building storage area, the chicken-wire
clutching at what it can. I have all-but

perfected extricating it, like the board game
Operation. I am a bike-removal surgeon,
carrying it down the internal corridor, only
banging against the chicken-wired sides
a number of times countable on the fingers

of the hands. I have almost perfected
the shrieking as the rain comes in, and we
abandon the e-bike and goose flap a kilometre
to the bus hub. The kid weighs more than
a box of books, but I hoist him to the apex

of the waterski pyramid that is my shoulders
and deploy him as an umbrella. Well
a counterweight, ballast, as the bus passes us
and I gallop, kid about the shoulders clutching
handfuls of my hair not for ballast but for

the music of this imperfect shrieking,
to the lights. The bus is loading, so I jink
across the red-lit crossing, kid aloft,
terrifying the oncoming buses but with such
pace and enough hooting of WAIT! to make

the number 7 before the door wheels shut.
Aboard the double decker up high
and at the glassy front we discuss matters and
things of the kind fathers and sons ruminate on
and nudge at. Things it would be a grave

shattering of decorum to reveal beyond
the circle of that sacred bond or some shit.
Shit, which he calls 'the es-aitch word', and
the mind forms the word in its totality: 'shit'.
To say 'the es-aitch word' is to form the word

'shit' in your listener's mind. But we discuss in
our braying voices these matters of these as I said
kinds and the co-inhabitants of the upper deck
shield their ears from our booms and squeaks
and off-colour ponderings and edgings beyond

the taboos etiquette would quietly prefer.
We hold no bar and bar no holds when it comes
to gore. Eyeballs stretched out of heads like
intestines, kneecaps popping, we bray it all
like asses. Also the word we are using now

in place of 'arses'. The bus lurches and winds.
The bus rumbles at the succession of red lights
on Victoria Street for weeks without end. Then
I must in the ideal zipped compartment
of my backpack produce two Eclipse mints,

a daily bribe, the punishment for non-payment
of which is disappointment and a shake
of the head that will come to mind in twenty
years and I will shudder like a whippet
in the snow. In the best of all possible zipped

compartments, the Eclipse mint tin would
reveal itself. The ideal zipped compartment
a notion, an incarnation of the abstract sublime.

When the compartment reveals only old
receipts and a broken set of sunglasses,

I pedal quickly. The bus makes a graunch,
the way a goose might graunch if it was more
double-decked and bussish. I pedal fast,
defeating the moment with a pin before it
balloons. I pitch up my apology just so, lacing it

with promises of the exciting things
that will make up for this dereliction of mints.
They must occur later today. Any further
pushed into the unknowable future
will be laughable. Nothing is as distant and

impossible as Thursday. The promise is confident.
Unquestionable! Any quaver in the confidence
is a one-way trip to hospital town
in a broken ambulance. Swung up before
the absence of Eclipse mints even enters

the mind, the apology must be pitched true
and moved on from like a swift. And we are
back to the routines and hee-hawing
asswards. Moved on from at such a clip like
the way I mentioned the swift just now and you

had no chance to groan at the brick-bat
wordplay. The bus rounds a curve on a lean.
Once, yet to be ensconced in the scurrying of
fatherdom, I scoffed at wordplay. Now, we
clutch to wordplay like leeches, sucking on

its pus and blood with our tongues out long.
We jabber at it. We gibber at it drooling.
On and on the bus clanks and concertinas.
Our gibberish paused by the blinding sun on
Cleveland Street, we thrash hands towards

the zipped compartment for the broken
sunglasses. For one of us the relief
announces itself in an exhale, the other,
guzzling at the fountain of the fatherdom
that is martyrdom, sighs at the sigh, though

the sun's lasers sear into his retinae.
The bus rises like the febrile dawn
over the hill, pausing the way only dawn can
for road works or to let some oncoming
other bus squeeze through. Slammed

by the kid's hammer hand, the button makes
its ding-dong and we veer into the stop,
scuttling down the steps and out the door
like father-and-his-son cockroaches.
We do not leave our bags aboard every time,

and not this time, and with minutes to spare
his legs run him out of sight into school.
I swivel in a slump towards the bus stop
back the way
we came to

abseil down
the winding
hill to town

and work only
twenty minutes

late, the bus
quieter
now, secret and unheard in myself, while
others chitter, to the delight of my unuttered
judgements. Arriving at my desk somehow

clutching coffee – not clutching just coffee, that
would burn the hand and stain the pant-leg,
but a hideous KeepCup of it – I am aged.
I am here for work as aged as the night sky
and this is how half the week

in a saga I have wound myself here, okay.

The Bumblebee Poem Writes Itself

. . . the whole hive at it, their cooperative
consciousness fuzzing at the keyboard,
rounded bee bums depressing keys.

Another one at the delete erases it all.
The bumblebee poem unwrites itself
to the relief of much waggling.

Not only bumblebee bums waggle, you think.
Human bums waggle too. But the bee bum
waggle means more, if only to bees

and entomologists. *The rain hisses.*
The rain paddles us with its pitilessness,
the bumblebees write, their patter petty.

Waterproof Dictator

My best ideas came to me
at night.
So I learned to pull out

the dictation app
and read them straight in.
My best ideas decided

to come to me in the shower.
You can't have this,
my best ideas say.

These best ideas are special.
They're not for other people.
So I'm inventing a . . .

[video loops]

Dress Code

Your outfit is not a calamity.
No one will ask if you bought it at a farmers market.

Your face does not clash with your shoes.
You could totally fuck your way out of a morgue in that.

People still wear this kind of thing.
You clearly get that style is not something you cut out

of a *National Geographic*
with hedge clippers.

No one thinks you are slut-shaming yourself.
Not an eyesore!

No face will involuntarily crumple
as if it had smelt your gym bag.

None of us would have the right to sneer

and then complain that it was your fault,

that you are making us feel bad about ourselves

as tolerant and kind people
with something so overpoweringly hideous.

Nobody could rightfully ask if you got dressed in the dark
in the mid-2000s

while holding on to an electric fence.

Your arse is not wrong.

No one is asking what those pants stains are.
Your ears are not weird.

Do you look like a bookcase bought from the Warehouse?
Queen Midas, whose touch causes virginity?

A swamp mutant in a thistle patch?
None of the above.

Opulence

It's very simple, very plain. Understated.
Just the single diamond
on each ear. Little blood-drop diamonds.
Not blood diamonds. Darling!
More poor-to-average-health-and-safety diamonds.
They're working on it. They have a three-year plan.
But I have a friend, unrelatedly,
whose charity offsets the toil.
You buy the diamonds and offset the indentured

servitude and tragedy at 15%,
which goes to real work in the field
to call for higher standards
and highlight the bad actors and so on.
They threw a gala I thought excellent.
I have this elegant little award. Understated. Sleek.
I'm holding it, reflecting on your concerns
with my head tilted to the window,
the silver light catching the diamonds just so.

But I will note them down
in this unassuming little soft-touch notebook.
Remember pony-hair leather?
It was a sensation on the fingers.
Ruined by the horse-meat scandal was Sophie's theory.
She has on a simple dress. Understated silhouette.
Nothing gauche or gaudy.
Often the poor have a style I admire.
Plain, unfussy, home-made.

Synonyms for Vag

You need to know I know. That even at
this first line – look, I've gone on to a second,
well perhaps then not – *I know.* I'd reckoned
it was fine to blurt, the heart on sleeve and that
was something of a virtue, like at – well gosh –
her launch, informing Talia,
like some cold-blood *Rhynchocephalia*,
she'd cried so much her make-up was awash.
I walked that line oblivious. But you,
ten years ago, a lunchtime pub for Scrabble,
you, an intern, asked. Without pre-babble
or a thought I shot to the taboo.
You squirmed. 'What's "quim"?' At hand were minimums
but, 'Pussy!' I'd replied, rejecting synonyms.

JUST AD NAUSEUM

Do You Wish to Continue?

(as said by the self-checkout machines)

Do you wish to continue pepper-spraying my earholes with your raspberries of tutting?

Do you wish to continue sending me the same email with the words in ever more preposterous rearrangements but saying the same thing, louder and louder, until every letter is a cap, bold, ultrabold, filling the entire screen, filling so much of the screen you can see just the edge of a bullet point?

Do you wish to continue, your face like a gibbon's – AAAH – overacting surprise?

Do you wish to continue like a somersaulting robot dog?

Do you wish to continue cancanning into the same lift, the door closing on your coffee, a shark trying to nibble a blueberry?

Do you wish to continue when we are all blueberries under the enormous thumb of time, each awaiting our meek squishing?

Do you wish to continue squirming like a mortal?

Do you wish to continue writhing like a photocopier jam?

Do you wish to continue hurtling on your rent-a-scooter through the death stares of Christmas pedestrians like you've pre-coated your opinions in Teflon?

Do you wish to continue scrolling? You can't say doomscrolling anymore – too on the nose – like cowabunga I'm fresh. You can't say anything anymore, apart from 'you can't say anything anymore', and you do, all the time, and you say everything. Every little thing.

Do you wish to continue sleepwalking backwards up the spiral staircase in the carpark to hell?

Do you wish to continue? Do you *wanna* continue? Canoe Wānaka, can you? Don't know what fish can win you? Do you wink and canoodle? Like a newt in a tutu? Like a pig in a pick 'n' mix? Do you really really really? Wanna? Zig-a-zig . . . ?

AAAH.

Which 1990s Pin-Up Is Our Future Husband?

(After Morgan Bach, with permission)

A *Dolly* quiz can choose which beautiful
boy star is ours. To whom do we belong?
No form-class schoolbag boy is suitable,
their eyes not soft, nor jawlines strong.
Whose sweet-faced heart robs ours? Which heartthrob's wife,
or flop-haired singer's, will we be? Unless . . .
We're drawn towards the boys with stunted life
lines, beautiful dead boys we dare address
at séances slept over. River, Kurt,
or boys whose eyes deflect the glint of doom,
like grinning bad-good Heath, disguising hurt.
Keanu, Patrick, boys still yet to bloom,
their bromance never left to run its course,
nor ours: no wedding, scandal and divorce.

**

And though boywatching, there was Julia,
atop a table – hmm, peculiar –
or Gwen Stefani, Nat Imbruglia.

Tell Me Less

The years divulge more and more about the meat robot

I seem to be. The news is mostly bad surprises.
At six, I learned that I go peely-wally and faint,
that I'm squeamish at a blood level over
the thought of the robot's inner meat.

A chunk, a drop, a transition in colours.

The thinking isn't upset, the blood itself is.
I fainted in primary school, fainted at Scouts,
fainted during a video on menstruation
in fourth form science. At the dentist, at the urologist.

Once, inhaling nitrous with Niki and a sly barman,
I overlooked oxygen for a time and passed out,
awoke with my legs spasming.
'Take it easy,' said Niki.

But the years had divulged

something fresh. That I may spasm.
At fifteen it was migraines. First the aura on the right,
small sparks that expand to plasmatic noodles,
then a hole where the finger disappears as you

run it across. A pincer-like headache follows
and a few days shuddering from bright light.
One came during choir, the tenor line fritzing,
struggling home at a gallop, the cars popping

into view as I vaulted roads.

One before having to bus head-in-hands
up to Brooklyn and rescue my son from school.
One in a Teams meeting last week, instantly cancelled
to the certain relief of us both.

On my eighteenth birthday it was sexual dysfunction,
assorted bits of the robot miscalibrated,
and mutilated, to my eyes, in the attempt.
For thoroughness, after she had fled,

I fainted four times attempting to right

the apparatus. At twenty, impotence.
For each disclosure of the robot's meatworks,
however dizzied one may be
for a twinkling of hours, the news embeds

and we roll to the next.
Most of the conveyor belt of self-knowledge gestures
towards the way one comes across – the personality –
how much one might be one way or another,

a bore or a delight, how warm

or patronising, how large one's self-absorption
or how small one's common humanity,
but that's half-knowledge. The unknowable shape
in others' minds. Deniable. The meatworks

are harder to rebut. Two years ago at forty-eight,
fainting again, this time an episode,

not triggered by the blood's disgust of itself,
but some poisonous imbalance,

I was vomiting as I came to. Alone at home,

in the carpeted corridor, peely-wally, unable
to stand, far from my phone, metres
from the unreachable bathroom, and
blacking out a second time, I continued vomiting.

Some while unconscious, some in the madness
of coming to. Coming to is slow. Thoughts are a boil,
but you are trying to grip them.
Your eyes open to a place, not your bed,

not a hotel bed, not a place it makes sense to be,

and you are vomiting out your nose
onto the carpet, and alone.
Like every family there is dementia
and cancer in mine. Conditions one will come to

and reel from then bear.
This week it wasn't those, something fresh,
rather, and the usual bad surprise.
The meat robot is not ready to reveal its new frailty.

But at fifty, I have inserted anaesthetic

suppositories high into places I was unaware of
and feel the rolling on ahead,

diminished too, naturally. And for all the blood,
and the reeling at the blood level,

I did not faint.

The Jaw Is a Face Bone

See how it flaps? Good for chewing
or issuing directions.
Go along a street. After some time take a turn.
Take a few more turns at specific points,
and in specific bearings, left or right or east. Then
when you see a thing
I am mumbling the name of but you're
too polite to ask me to repeat, follow
a little further, and there you are,
very near the velodrome. Just
wind along some more, feeling it,
trusting your gut, your legs, feeling it
deep in your sense of direction,
deep in the inner map of the mind's eye,
a bird's eye, I think of it as, like a duck or emu,
but you may have a different mind animal,
a mole from the look of you-no-offence-I-like-moles.
Ignore wrong paths and tempting
distractions, such as, as an example,
an object of a specific type,
animate or inanimate
that you might want to conduct
some sort of business with, say, drinking it,
but not that.
Ignore any cats in top hats.
There will be none,
or few, so that one is unhelpfully clear.
And there you are at the discothèque.

Greg

(for Stacey, or originally for Stacey but then for Greg, or Greg as well)

Greg gets out of his Prius like a lumberjack.
Greg makes a little noise when
he disagrees with you but doesn't
want to get into it.

Greg's doing the crossword in frameless
spectacles and a jazzy shirt.
Greg is Aslan in a C.S. Lewis dramatisation.
Roaring Greg!

Stacey said, 'Greg,' at a gathering, but
I had misoverheard her.
She was in bits.
Laughing.

What was it about? No one should
laugh at Gregs I thought.
Gregs are vital.
The whole mechanism falls apart without

the Greg.
Gregs are symbolic: of kindness,
of a skew-whiff mane,
of stay-at-home-daddom.

The Greg is theatrically unshowy.
The Greg is proud.
I resolve to chastise Stacey with a poem.
But I have misoverheard her.

She said, 'Hummus,' or 'Thanks, Morgan,' or
something that when I asked,
'Did you say, Greg?' it didn't make sense.
'When?'

Greg gets his brother a glass of
water to soothe the hangover.
Greg entertains his nephew so that
his brother can wince in peace.

I wince in peace.
Greg ferries his nephew
and brother to the airport.
Greg gets out of his Prius like a lumberjack,

circles to the back and hoists
out the suitcase.
Later in the day, up north, his brother is
at a gathering.

'Greg,' says Stacey, then she's in bits.
Who is this Greg? I wonder.
This never-actually-said Greg?
Greg, Stacey. Stacey, Greg.

I Lost My Wardrobe in the War

I lost my leg in the war.
I lost my hair
in the war.
I lost my wallet
on a bus

in the war.
I lost my sense of humour
in the war.
I lost my dignity in the war.
I lost my convictions,

and the shame of losing my convictions.
I lost my sense of geometry in the
war.
I lost my house, my livelihood,
my children, the shirt

off my back, everything
but my underpants,
in the war.
I found something though,
something that could sustain me,

through cold wind
and twilights of terror,
something small and true
that I could hold to
in the weakest moments, even

sleep-starved and blindfolded,

yet I lost that too

in the war.

Notes

'Thing': I genuinely wrote this by stitching together late-night pronouncements muttered into my dictation app. I first read a version in Warrington at an event organised by Richard Reeve (thanks), and realised it needed to make more sense. Not sure it does. John Ashbery wrote a lot of great first lines that his poems then tried to make sense of with varying results. Fact check: I am not Oscar Wilde.

'Pastiche for Mum': I wrote this for, and read it at, Mum's funeral in 2022. I had choked up before reading it, but pushed on through and got a good laugh. The guilty funeral laugh is to be prized. Yes it's a pastiche of all the lines in Clare Harner's famous funeral poem 'Immortality' ('Do not stand / By my grave, and weep. / I am not there, / I do not sleep –'), a poem that at times I grudgingly admire but also loathe.

'Fair-Weather Friend': Niki Ward was my best friend. We'd seen less of each other in the last twenty years, but her death still hurts me. Thanks to the crowd at the Pegasus reading who were there to hear me sob and read it just a week after she'd died. Poetry not without uses after all. 'So Fresh, So Clean' by Outkast and 'Work It' by Missy Elliott are the two songs mentioned.

'Old Farts': Names altered but if you know you know and don't sue me please.

'Pig Magnet': Ever since writing this title I imagined it having a note to explain itself. The only reason I stuck with the title was knowing that a note would somehow anchor its absolute inaptness. It is meaningless. I just thought it sounded funny. Pigs as in cops? Like 'chick magnet' but for attractors of douchebags? Pigs as in delighted diners? Swine? I don't know.

'Dress Code' and 'Opulence': I wrote these trying to write a poem to perform at my ex-wife Kate's fortieth birthday party. The party's theme was 'opulence', but I worried that the 'Opulence' poem sounded mean so I wrote 'Dress Code'. Again, it is mean, but the kind of mean humour I reckoned or hoped Kate would like. I think I walked the line. But did I?

'Which 1990s Pin-Up Is Our Future Husband': OK, so Morgan Bach was doing a LitCrawl event with a sonnet theme and she was feeling iffy on that. I had bragged that I could turn anything she wrote into a sonnet. It was win-win for us both. Morgan's kinda coming-out poem was inappropriate in my hands, but man I loved trying to write this. Morgan's original is better.

Acknowledgements

The usual suspects need acknowledging. My gut says they need apologising to also, but my gut is a hand-wringing little creep. If you are bothering to read these acknowledgments, chances are high that you expect to appear here. Be ready to grunt in recognition or tut in rage. If you are reading them due to some compulsion for completeness, having ground your way through all the poems, and why stop there, then thank you. Thank you, most of all. If no such person exists, and you have not in fact read this, then I thank you nonetheless, kind and imagined entity.

The publishing team will have felt obliged to read this far, just in the instance that I have slipped in something libellous or misspelled. I thank all at Te Herenga Waka University Press with non-faux earnestness! Thank you, Always Becominging! Such a kind and thoughtful edit. Thank you Fergus Barrowman! Thank you Caoimhe McKeogh! Thank you, especially, Ashleigh Young. Yes, as the hovering second editor, but mostly for being my dearest friend and laughing dutifully at my jokes. May all your hedges be drunken.

Usual suspects time. I have failed to send poems to magazines in the last couple years, but I still spammed all and randomly sundry, or worse read aloud at you. Thanks to Morgan Bach, Louise Cooper, Jon Cox, Emma Neale, James McNaughton, Peter Ward, Richard Reeve, Cilla McQueen, David Kārena-Holmes, Michael Steven, James Brown, Stacey Teague, Blair Reeve, Talia Marshall, Rebecca Hawkes, Katherine Dolan, Kate Wanwimolruk, Kushana Bush and Andy Paterson. Even my son Ames had to listen to some and he gets a shred of thanks too.

Others at Poetry Club will now be thanked for contributing vibewise: the poems you found and read have inspired me (to steal their ideas). Cheers Dani Yourukova, Ash Davida Jane, Ella Borrie, Leah Dodd, Hannah Mettner, Chris Tse, Francis Cooke, Alayne Dick, Una Cuickshank, others already mentioned and all the lurkers on the chat.

Two poems appeared in issues of *Landfall*, 'The Drunken Hedge' and 'Another Poem with a Found Feather': thanks Lynley Edmeades. The former poem also appeared in *Newsroom* (Reading Room): thanks Steve Braunias. 'Do You Wish to Continue?' was written for the 2023 winter solstice event on Island Bay beach, organised by (tips hat) Andrew Laking. Thanks to Joan Fleming who made her class read a poem of mine, which inspired me to write its sequel, 'Pig Magnet', and I read that to them, while discovering it was very very long. Thanks also to Therese Lloyd, who set up the Gen-X reading at Te Papa, where I first read the title poem to this collection.

Thanks Todd Atticus for the cover and for launching my little avatar to his untimely demise. It is not at all what he would've wanted, but boohoo too bad. I love it.